OUR
DAY OUT

WILLY RUSSELL

Introduction and questions by
Tim Bezant

Heinemann

Inspiring generations

Heinemann is an imprint of Pearson Education Limited,
a company incorporated in England and Wales, having
its registered office at Edinburgh Gate, Harlow, Essex, CM20 2JE.
Registered company number: 872828

First published in 1987 by Hutchinson Education
First published in the *Heinemann Plays* series 1993

32

A catalogue record for this book is available from the British Library on request.
ISBN: 978 0 435233 01 3

CONTENTS

PREFACE

In this edition of *Our Day Out*, you will find notes, questions and activities to help in studying the play in class, particularly at GCSE level.

The introduction provides background information on the author and the circumstances which led to the conception of this play.

The activities at the end of the book range from straight-forward *Keeping Track* questions which can be tackled at the end of each scene to focus close attention on what is happening in the play, through more detailed work on characters and themes in *Explorations,* to more advanced discussion questions under *Criticism.* This is followed by suggestions for reading further plays by Willy Russell as well as an in-depth study of the playwright.

INTRODUCTION

Willy Russell

Willy Russell was born on August 23rd, 1947 in Whiston, Lancashire. He grew up in Knowsley, a model village set in the countryside outside Liverpool. His father worked for Imperial Chemicals before leaving to run his own chip shop. Russell attended Woolfall Secondary School for one year, later describing it as 'chaotic, badly run', and Rainford Secondary School, which he left at the age of fifteen with no formal qualifications.

Thereafter, he worked as a ladies' hairdresser for five years and as a labourer for a further year. During this time he was also singing semi-professionally in a group in the folk music clubs in and around Liverpool, as well as following evening classes. He then enrolled on a one year 'A' level course which enabled him to go to St Katherine's College of Higher Education in Liverpool in 1970 in order to train as a teacher.

It was in March 1971, having already tried his hand at writing music, songs, poetry and even a novel that Russell discovered he wanted to be a playwright when he attended a performance of a play entitled *Unruly Elements* at Liverpool's Everyman Theatre. This play took ordinary Liverpool people as its characters and showed Russell he could use his own experiences in his own writing. His first play, *Keep your Eyes Down*, about a young factory worker who wants success in the music business, was presented in December 1971 by St Katherine's College Drama Society.

From then on, Russell worked semi-professionally as a playwright while following his course at college. His play, *King of the Castle*, was presented on BBC2 in 1973. Once he had qualified as a teacher he worked at Shorefields Comprehensive School in Liverpool, where his experiences would lead directly into the writing of *Our Day Out*. However, he kept his teaching job only until 1974 when the success of his play *John, Paul, George, Ringo and Bert*, a play with music about the Beatles, led to its transferring from the Everyman Theatre in Liverpool to the Lyric Theatre in London's West End for a year. As a result of this, Russell was able to devote himself to writing full-time.

Russell's most successful plays since then have been linked by the twin themes of choice and escape. *Breezeblock Park* (Liverpool 1975, London 1977) is a play about working-class family life in Liverpool, in which one of the members of the family attempts to break away from its confines. *Our Day Out* (first televised in 1977 and made into a musical in 1983) follows a school trip from an inner-city school to the zoo and the seaside; and *Stags and Hens* (Liverpool 1978, London 1987, later filmed as *Dancing thru the Dark*) focuses upon the ladies' and gents' cloakrooms at a Liverpool night club at which, unknown to each other, a couple to be married the next day are having their final parties as single people. In all of these plays, Russell uses natural Liverpool humour and characters to communicate his more serious content to his audience.

Perhaps Russell's most famous play, however, is *Educating Rita*, which was written for the Royal Shakespeare Company in 1980 and ran in London at the Piccadilly Theatre for over two years. It was filmed in 1983, starring Julie Walters in the rôle of Rita, a Liverpool hairdresser who is dissatisfied with her life, marriage and social background and wants to escape this closed situation. To do so she enrols in an Open University English Degree course and, by successfully taking her degree, achieves both independence and the right to choose what she will do with her life. Again, the humour of the play arises from the interaction between characters from contrasting backgrounds and, again, Russell's serious theme arises through the humour.

His most recent plays are *Blood Brothers* (1983) and *Shirley Valentine* (1986). *Blood Brothers* is a musical for which Russell wrote book, lyrics and music. It traces the lives of twin brothers separated at birth, who, ignorant of their brotherhood, become friends only to die together tragically. *Blood Brothers* started its second run of performances in London in 1988. *Shirley Valentine* was premiered at Liverpool Everyman in 1986, transferred to London in 1989 and has also been filmed. It is a one-woman show in which a bored Liverpool housewife leaves her home and husband for a holiday in Greece where, finding a degree of independence and freedom, she chooses to remain and live.

'To write a play', Willy Russell has written, 'one must passionately believe in something which one wants to communicate'. It is clear that in writing his plays Russell is passionately concerned with the plight of the individual – more often than not a woman – who craves freedom from a background or situation with which she finds herself out of sympathy. His characters and their situations are drawn from real-life, which Russell then refines with his warm, humorous sense of humanity to create believable, archetypal plays with which a wide-ranging audience can identify. In this respect, he is truly one of our most successful and popular playwrights.

Our Day Out

While *Our Day Out* was written in 1977, its roots are firmly planted in Russell's experiences at Shorefields Comprehensive School where he taught from 1973–4. In that year, Russell accompanied the teacher of the remedial department, Mrs Dorothy King, on a trip she ran to Conway Castle and Zoo for the children in her care. At the last minute, a disciplinarian Deputy Headteacher also joined the party, creating a potential recipe for disaster. During the course of the day, however, the Deputy Head relaxed and enjoyed himself, only to revert to his usual self at the end of the day. In doing so, he destroyed all the positive achievements of the day out.

Clearly, all the vital elements of Russell's play were implicit in this day. In writing his play, however, Russell does not simply tell the story of what happened. Rather, by presenting characters and a situation familiar to his audience, he created an archetypal situation representative of school trips of this nature which he then uses as a springboard for the serious questions he asks his audience.

At the core of the play lies the contrast between Mrs Kay and Mr Briggs and their respective educational philosophies. Mrs Kay is the teacher of the Progress Class and the leader of the day out. Her main concern is that the children should have an enjoyable day and, to that end, she is prepared to allow them to behave as they wish, so long as they also consider other people. Mr Briggs is the Deputy Headteacher who is sent on the trip at the last minute by the Headmaster. He is more concerned that the trip, which he has had no part in organising, should be an educational experience for the pupils and he is appalled both by Mrs Kay's attitude and her handling of the pupils. The clashes between the two characters in which each makes it clear what they think of the other and their values, create most of the tension in the play and serve to focus the audience's attention upon what type of education is most appropriate for this type of special needs pupil. These characters are, therefore, deliberately created as opposites to each other and, even after Mr Briggs has relaxed and enjoyed himself with Mrs Kay and her pupils at the funfair, upon their return to school it becomes clear that the day has done nothing to change him fundamentally.

None of the other adult characters are created in such detail. Colin and Susan, the younger teachers involved in the trip, are lovers whom the children seek to embarrass. This, in turn, leads to humorous confusion for Mr Briggs as Susan takes matters into her own hands. Ronny Suttcliffe, the coach driver, is a functional character who also provides the source of some comic relief, as do the shopkeepers, Mac and John, who inflate their prices as they see the coach approaching only to be (justifiably?) ill-treated as the children empty their shelves behind their backs.

The characters of the children in the Progress Class can also be broken down into archetypes. Reilly and Digga are the older, tougher boys, smoking a sly cigarette at the back of the coach and aggravating Colin and Susan until they – specifically Reilly – receive their come-uppance. Linda and Karen are evidently out to use the day in order to try and impress Colin (in both their dress and their attitude) for both have a crush on him. Milton, Andrews and Ronson are younger children whose function within the play is to provide light relief as and when they are picked on, although Ronson does reveal some intelligence when watching the bear in its pit. The character in the class with whom the audience identifies most is Carol Chandler, who is both the first and last character we meet. During the course of the day, it is Carol who grows into an understanding of her predicament: becoming aware of the fact that she is trapped into her social situation by virtue of her background and abilities, she leaves the group at the beach to climb the cliffs and, when Mr Briggs finds her, threatens to kill herself. While he saves her, and she is grateful for this, by the end of the play it is clear that the day has done nothing to alleviate Carol's situation. If anything, in giving her an understanding of its true nature, it may have made it worse.

Finally, the language of the pupils in the Progress Class is recognisably that of inner-city Liverpool: indeed, in the original BBC film of the play the Progress Class pupils were played by schoolchildren from Liverpool. Their use of slang and dialect would be matched by the local accent, and would contrast strongly with the Standard English spoken by their teachers. Much of the humour of the play arises from the gulf between the pupils and Mr Briggs and from their mutual incomprehension: it is also the source of its success, which serves to highlight the issue of the function of education and schooling for pupils such as those in the Progress Class.

Reading the Play and Presentation

All plays are written to be performed or, at the very least, read aloud. This is certainly true of *Our Day Out*, for only in reading the play aloud will the naturalistic, colloquial conversational nature of the play become fully clear. As the characters are heard, a fuller understanding of their attitudes and opinions, both of themselves and of others, can be formed. Arising from this, it becomes possible to develop a sense of how the characters would show their opinions and reactions in other, physical ways. It is only through an effective (and, if need be, rehearsed) reading of the play that an understanding of the various characters' backgrounds, natures and feelings can begin to be developed.

Our Day Out was conceived and written as a play for television. In watching it, we would watch the events of the play unfold against the exact backgrounds and in the particular environments demanded by the author, as the camera takes us to precisely those locations. In reading the play, therefore, it is vital that we think about the setting specified by Russell for each scene: how will the exterior of the school look? What sort of street will it be set in? What sort of coach is used for the trip? What type of scenery does it pass through, both in Liverpool and beyond? How will the scenery at the zoo, at the castle and at the beach be different to everything that has gone before? It is only by visualising the answers to these questions that the context for the action of the play can be created in our mind's eye.

The play is divided into forty-one shooting scenes: of these, some are longer sequences, such as Scene Six (set on the coach) while others are short, such as Scenes Ten and Eleven (as the coach arrives at the first café). In Scene Six, Russell is obviously taking the time to convey to the reader and viewer the events on the coach during what would be an hour's journey, and, in so doing, to add depth and detail to the characters involved, whereas in Scenes Ten and Eleven, which are necessarily short, he is paving the way for the humour in Scene Twelve (and sub-sequent scenes). Careful choice will lend particular scenes or extracts from scenes to detailed study and to reading and rehearsing in small groups. A useful approach is to read scenes or sections aloud first of all in order to understand the action and to discover the subtext, which reveals the changing reactions and opinions of the characters implicit in their dialogue in greater depth.

Following the play you will find two series of questions. *Keeping Track* is intended to help your understanding of the action and the characters as the play develops and can be used while reading the play for the first time. *Explorations* are more detailed and demanding questions organised according to characters, themes, presentation and criticism. The questions in this section may lead to coursework assignments or examination practice. All the questions are designed to stimulate knowledge, understanding and, hopefully, enjoyment of the play.

Tim Bezant

List of Characters

The Teachers:

MRS KAY (in her early forties)
SUSAN (early twenties)
COLIN (early twenties)
BRIGGS (early thirties)
HEADMASTER

The Kids:

CAROL (13)
REILLY (15)
DIGGA (15)
LINDA (15)
KAREN (15)
OTHER KIDS (all around 12 or 13)

ANDREWS (13)
RONSON (13)
KEVIN (12)
JIMMY (12)
MAURICE (12)

Other Adults:

LES, the 'lollipop man'
THE DRIVER
MRS ROBERTS
WAITRESS

JOHN
MAC
ANIMAL KEEPER
TWO OTHER ANIMAL KEEPERS

SCENE ONE **IN THE STREET**

The street is in the inner-city of Liverpool. KIDS *are streaming in one direction. It is approaching 9 a.m. The* KIDS *are pushing, shoving, rushing, ambling, leering and jeering. A group of older* KIDS *cross the road, ignoring the lollipop man's assistance. He points them out to a passing woman, obviously disgusted.* CAROL *rushes along the street wearing a school uniform which doubles as a street outfit and her Sunday best. She is eating half a sandwich and clutching a supermarket carrier bag. She arrives at the roadside and, as there isn't a vehicle in sight, goes to cross without bothering to enlist the aid of the lollipop man,* LES. *He stops her from stepping off the pavement.*

LES   'Ey you!

CAROL   (*stopping*) What?

LES   Come here. Come on!

CAROL   (*approaching him*) Agh ey, Les. Come on. I wanna get t' school.

LES   That makes a bloody change.

CAROL   We're goin' out. On a trip.

LES   Now listen. Are you listenin'? Y' don't cross the road without the assistance of the lollipop man. And that's me!

CAROL   There's nott'n comin', though.

LES   Now just you listen; I know it might look as though there's nothin' comin' but how do you know that a truck or car isn't gonna come speedin' out of that side road? Eh?

CAROL   (*looking*) Oh yeh. I never thought of that.

LES   No. I know y' didn't. Y' never do. None of y'. That's why the government hired me to look after y' all.

CAROL   Ta Les.

LES	Ey. Where y' goin' today then?
CAROL	It's somewhere far away. I forget.
LES	They all goin'?
CAROL	Only the kids who go the Progress Class.
LES	What's that?
CAROL	What? Y'don't know what the Progress Class is? It's Mrs Kay's class. Y' go down there in the week if y' can't do sums or writing. If y' backward like.
LES	By Christ, I'll bet she's kept busy. They're all bloody backward round here.
CAROL	I know. Come on Les. I wanna get there.
	LES *looks up and down the road. Not a vehicle in sight.*
LES	Just hold it there.
CAROL	There's nott'n comin'.
	(LES *looks down the road. In the distance a car is just appearing.*)
	Oh come on, Les.
	(LES *holds out his arm to prevent her from crossing. Only when the car is within striking distance does he walk out with his 'Stop' sign. The car pulls to a halt.* LES *waves* CAROL *across.*)
LES	(*quietly to* CAROL *as she passes*) I got him that time. Arrogant get that one is.
	CAROL *continues on her way. The driver of the car glares as* LES *waves him on.*

SCENE TWO **THE SCHOOL GATES**

A coach. Various groups of KIDS *are scattered nearby. One group surrounds a teacher,* MRS KAY, *all of them after her attention. Cries of, 'Miss, miss, miss, me mum said I could go, miss,' and 'Miss, can I come if I haven't got enough money?' and, 'Miss, can I come, miss?'*

MRS KAY All right, all right. Will you just let me have a minute's peace and I'll get you all sorted out. Right. Now those who've got permission to come on the trip but haven't yet paid, I want you to come over here.

(*She moves a short distance away and all the* KIDS *follow her.* BRIGGS *surveys this scene.*)

(*brightly*) Good morning, Mr Briggs.

BRIGGS (*begrudgingly*) Morning.

(*He turns and enters the school and addresses a couple of boys.*)

Come on, move!

SCENE THREE **THE HEADMASTER'S OFFICE**

The HEADMASTER *is talking to* BRIGGS, *who was the Driver of the car.*

HEADMASTER Well I'd like you to go with her, John. We can get Frank Collins to take over your examination classes for the day. I'd just like you to be there and keep an eye on things. I don't want to be unprofessional and talk about a member of staff but I get the impression she sees education as one long game.

BRIGGS Well ... if the antics in her department are anything to go by ... ! She always reminds me of a mother hen rather than a teacher ...

HEADMASTER Well, anyway, just try and keep things in some sort of order.

SCENE FOUR **THE SCHOOL GATES**

MRS KAY *is talking to two young teachers,* COLIN *and* SUSAN. *Around them are excited, lively* KIDS – *not lined up but in random groups.*

MRS KAY (*shouting to a* KID) Maurice! Come away from that road will you?

The KID *does so. Two older* KIDS *come rushing out of school and up to the* TEACHERS.

REILLY Miss ... miss, can we come wit' y'? Can we?

MRS KAY Oh, Brian! You know it's a trip for the Progress Class.

REILLY Agh, ay, miss, we used t' be in the Progress Class though.

SUSAN But you're not now, Brian. Now you can read and write you're back in normal classes.

MRS KAY Look Brian. You know I'd take you. But it's not up to me. Who's your form teacher?

REILLY Briggsy.

MRS KAY Well, you'll have to go and get his permission.

REILLY (*as he and* DIGGA *rush off*) You're ace, miss.

MRS KAY Brian!

(*He stops.*)

Bring a note.

REILLY (*worried*) Ah ... what for, miss?

MRS KAY (*smiling*) Because I wasn't born yesterday, Brian Reilly, and if I don't ask you for a note you'll just hide behind the corner for ten minutes and say he said you could go.

REILLY (*Knowing she's got him sussed.*) As if we'd do a thing like that, miss!

CAROL (*Tugging at* MRS KAY*'s arm.*) Where are we goin', miss?

MRS KAY Carol ... Miss Duncan's just told you. Conwy. We're going to Conwy.

CAROL Miss is that in England, eh?

COLIN It's in Wales, Carol.

CAROL Will we have t' get a boat?

MRS KAY Carol ... we're going on a coach. Look, it's there. You can get on now.

(She shouts out to the rest of the KIDS.*)*

Go on … you can all get on now.

There is a wild rush of KIDS *to the coach doors. The* DRIVER *appears and blocks the way.*

DRIVER   Right. Just stop there. Don't move.

KID   Miss said we could get on.

DRIVER   Oh, did she now?

KIDS   Yeh.

DRIVER   Well, let me tell youse lot something now. Miss isn't the driver of this coach. I am. An' if I say y' don't get on, y' don't get on.

MRS KAY   Is anything wrong, Driver?

DRIVER   Are these children in your charge, madam?

MRS KAY   Yes.

DRIVER   Well y' haven't checked them, have y'?

MRS KAY   Checked them? Checked them for what?

DRIVER   Chocolate an' lemonade! We don't allow it. I've seen it on other coaches madam; fifty-two vomitin' kids … it's no joke. No, I'm sorry, we don't allow that.

MRS KAY   *(to* SUSAN*)* Here comes Mr Happiness. All right, Driver … I'll check for you.

(to KIDS*)*

… Now listen, everyone. If anybody's got any chocolate or lemonade I want you to put your hands up.

(A sea of dumb faces and unraised hands. MRS KAY *smiles at the* DRIVER.*)*

There you are, Driver. All right?

DRIVER   No, it's not all right. Y' can't just take their word for it. They have to be searched. Y' can't just believe kids.

Pause. MRS KAY *stares at him. She could blow up but she doesn't.*

MRS KAY	Can I have a word with you, Driver, in private?

(Reluctantly the DRIVER *gets off the coach and goes across to her. She manoeuvres it so that he has his back to the coach and the* KIDS.)

What's your name, Driver?

DRIVER	Me name? I don't usually have to give me name.
MRS KAY	Oh, come on … what's your name?
DRIVER	Suttcliffe, Ronny Suttcliffe.
MRS KAY	Well, Ronny (*pointing*), take a look up these streets.

(He does and she motions the other teachers to be getting the KIDS *on the coach.)*

Ronny, would you say they were the sort of streets that housed prosperous parents?

DRIVER	We usually only do the better schools.
MRS KAY	All right, you don't like these kids. I can tell that. But do you have to cause them so much pain?
DRIVER	(*shocked*) What have I done? I only told 'em to wait …
MRS KAY	Ronny, the kids with me today don't know what it is to *look* at a bar of chocolate. Lemonade never touches their lips. (*We almost hear the violins.*) These are the children, Ronny, who stand outside shop windows in the pouring rain, looking and longing and never getting. Even at Christmas, at Christmas-time when your kids from the better schools are opening presents and singing carols, these kids are left to wander the cold cruel streets.

Pause as she sees the effect she is having. The DRIVER *is grief-stricken.*

SCENE FIVE **INSIDE THE COACH**

The KIDS *are stuffing themselves with sweets and lemonade. The* DRIVER *comes on board and by the time he turns to face the* KIDS *there is not a bottle of lemonade or chocolate bar in sight. The* DRIVER *puts his hand into his pocket and pulls out a note.*

DRIVER   Here you are, son (*to* KID *in front seat*), run over to the shops an' get what sweets y' can with that.

The KID *takes the money and gets off the coach.* SUSAN, *the young teacher, leans across to* MRS KAY.

SUSAN   What did you do?

MRS KAY   Lied like hell, of course!

(She gets up and faces the KIDS.*)*

Now, will you listen everyone. We'll be setting off for Conwy in a couple of minutes.

(*cheers*)

Now listen! We want everyone to enjoy themselves, so let's have no silly squabbling or doing anything that might be dangerous to yourselves or to others. That's the only rule we have today: think of yourselves, but think of others as well.

REILLY *and* DIGGA *rush into the bus.*

REILLY   Miss, miss, we're coming' wit' y', miss. He said it's all right.

MRS KAY   Brian, where's the note?

REILLY   He didn't give us one, miss. He's comin' himself. He said to wait.

DIGGA *and* REILLY *go to the back of the coach.* MRS KAY *looks at* COLIN *and* SUSAN.

COLIN   He's coming to keep an eye on us.

SUSAN   Make sure we don't enjoy ourselves.

MRS KAY   Ah well. We'll just have to deal with him the best way we can.

She sits down next to CAROL. *On the back seat of the coach* REILLY *and* DIGGA *are facing some small* KIDS.

REILLY   Right, dickheads. Move!

LITTLE KID Why?

REILLY Cos we claimed the back seat, that's why.

LITTLE KID You're not even in the Progress though.

DIGGA We used to be though, so move.

REILLY Yeh. Respect y'elders!

At the front of the coach, BRIGGS *is climbing aboard. He stands at the front and stares and glares. The* KIDS *sigh – he is a cloud on the blue horizon.*

BRIGGS (*suddenly barks*) Reilly. Dickson. Sit down!

REILLY Sir, we was only …

BRIGGS (*staccato*) Sit down, now, come on, move!

(REILLY *and* DIGGA *sit on the two small* KIDS *who move to make room for them.*)

Go on, sort yourselves out!

(*He leans across to* MRS KAY *and speaks quietly.*)

You've got some real bright sparks here, Mrs Kay. A right bunch.

MRS KAY Well, I think we'll be safe now that you've come to look after us.

BRIGGS (*Looking at the* KIDS.) There's a few of 'em I could sling off right now.

MRS KAY Oh, you are coming with us then?

BRIGGS The Boss thought it might be a good idea if you had an extra member of staff.

(*Stands to address the* KIDS.)

Right, listen.

(*pause*)

We don't want you to think that we don't want you to enjoy yourselves today, because we do! But a lot of you haven't been on a school visit before so you won't know *how* to enjoy yourselves. So I'll tell you. To enjoy a coach trip we sit in our seats. We don't wander up and down the aisle. We talk quietly to our neighbour, not shout at our mates four seats down. (*staccato*) Are you listening, girl! We look nicely out of the windows at the scenery. And we don't do anything else.

(*Throughout the speech the* KIDS *look disappointed.*)

Don't worry, I've driven in my car behind school coaches and seen it. A mass of little hands raised in two-fingered gestures to the passing cars. Yes. But we won't do that will we? Will we?

Chorus of: 'No sir.'

BRIGGS No, sir. We won't.

The KID *returning from the shop, armed with sweets, climbs on to the bus.*

KID I've got them ... I've got loads ...

BRIGGS Where've you been?

KID Gettin' sweets, sir.

BRIGGS Sweets?

MRS KAY (*Reaching for sweets.*) Thank you, Maurice.

BRIGGS Sweets?

The DRIVER *taps* BRIGGS *on the shoulder.*

DRIVER Excuse me, can I have a word with you, please?

BRIGGS (*puzzled*) Yes.

The DRIVER *gets off the coach and* BRIGGS *follows.* MRS KAY *gives the sweets to* SUSAN *who starts to dish them out. We hear a snatch of the* DRIVER*'s speech to* BRIGGS.

DRIVER The thing is, about these kids, they're like little souls lost an' wanderin' the cruel heartless streets ...

Inside the coach, COLIN *has joined* SUSAN *in giving out the sweets.* COLIN *is at the back seat.*

REILLY How y' gettin' on with miss, eh sir?

DIGGA We saw y', sir, goin' into that pub with her, sir.

SUSAN *is watching in the background.*

COLIN   (*Covering his embarrassment.*) Did you?

REILLY   Are you in love with her, sir? Are y'?

COLIN   (*Making his escape.*) All right … you've all got sweets have you?

REILLY   Sir's in love, sir's in love!

       REILLY *laughs and jeers as* COLIN *makes his way down the aisle.*

SUSAN   Watch it, Brian!

REILLY   (*feigned innocence*) What?

SUSAN   You know what.

REILLY   Agh ey, he is in love with y' though, isn't he, miss.

DIGGA   Miss, I'll bet he wants t' marry y'.

REILLY   You'd be better off with me, miss. I'm better lookin'. An' I'm sexier!

SUSAN   (*Giving up playing it straight. She goes up to him, leans across and whispers.*) Brian … little boys shouldn't try to act like men. The day might come when their words are put to the test!

       She walks away.

REILLY   (*jeering*) Any day, miss … any day …

       He laughs.

DIGGA   What did she say? What did she say?

REILLY   Said she fancied me.

       At the front of the coach, BRIGGS *and the* DRIVER *are climbing back on board.* BRIGGS *sits opposite* MRS KAY. *He leans across to her.*

BRIGGS   (*quietly*) We've got a right head case of a driver.

       The engine roars into life. The KIDS *cheer.* BRIGGS *turns round with a warning look as the coach pulls away from the school. Thousands of little fingers raise in a V-sign out of the windows.*

SCENE SIX **LEAVING THE CITY**

As the coach goes along the city streets the KIDS *are talking and laughing and pointing. On the back seat,* REILLY *secretly takes out a packet of cigarettes. The* LITTLE KID *sees them.*

DIGGA Reilly, light up.

REILLY Where's Briggsy?

DIGGA He's at the front, I'll keep dixie. Come on, we're all right, light up.

LITTLE KID Agh 'ey. You've got ciggies. I'm gonna tell miss.

REILLY Shut up you an' open that friggin' window.

LITTLE KID No ... I'm gonna tell miss.

DIGGA Go'n tell her. She won't do nott'n anyway.

LITTLE KID I'll tell sir.

REILLY You do an' I'll gob y'.

DIGGA Come on ... open that window, you.

LITTLE KID Why?

REILLY Why d' y' think? So we get a bit of fresh air.

LITTLE KID Well there's no fresh air round here. You just wanna smoke. An' smokin' stunts y' growth.

REILLY I'll stunt your friggin' growth if y' don't get it open.

ANDREWS *gets up and reaches for the window.*

ANDREWS I'll open it for y' Reilly.

REILLY *ducks behind the seat and lights up.*

ANDREWS Gis a ciggy.

REILLY Get y' own ciggies.

ANDREWS Ah go on. I opened the window for y'.

DIGGA Y' can buy one off us.

ANDREWS I can't. I haven't got any money.

REILLY Course y've got money.

ANDREWS Me ma wouldn't give me any. She didn't have any.

DIGGA   Go 'way … your ma's loaded.

ANDREWS   No she's not.

REILLY   Well she should be … all the fellers she picks up on Parly.

ANDREWS   Go on … gis a ciggy.

DIGGA   She's always with the blacks off the boats, your ma. And they're loaded, them blacks are.

REILLY   An' you must have money cos they pay a fortune for a bit of White.

ANDREWS   Well *I've* got no money … honest.

DIGGA   Well, y've got no ciggies either.

ANDREWS   I'll give y' half me sarnies for one ciggie.

REILLY   What's on 'em?

ANDREWS   Jam.

REILLY   I hate jam.

They have become lax about keeping an eye out and do not notice BRIGGS *getting up from his seat and approaching the back of the coach.* DIGGA *suddenly looks up and sees him.*

DIGGA   Briggs!

REILLY *passes the cigarette to* ANDREWS.

REILLY   Here!

ANDREWS   Ta.

ANDREWS *takes it and, making sure that his head is out of sight, he takes a huge drag. When he looks up,* BRIGGS *is peering down at him.*

BRIGGS   Put it out!

ANDREWS   Sir, sir, I wasn't …

BRIGGS   Put it out. Now get to the front of the coach.

ANDREWS   Sir, I was just …

BRIGGS   I said get to the front!

(ANDREWS *sighs, gets up and goes to the front of the*

coach. BRIGGS *sits in* ANDREWS' *seat.*)

Was it your ciggie, Reilly?

REILLY   Sir, I swear on me mother.

DIGGA   Don't believe him, sir. How can he swear on his mother. She's been dead for ten years.

BRIGGS   All right, all right. We don't want any argument. There'll be no more smoking if I stay up here, will there?

CAROL, who is sitting next to MRS KAY, *is staring out of the window.*

CAROL   Isn't it horrible, eh, miss.

MRS KAY   Mm?

CAROL   Y' know … all the thingy like. The dirt an' that.

(pause) I like them nice places.

MRS KAY   Which places?

CAROL   Y' know them places on the telly. Where they have gardens an' trees outside an' that.

MRS KAY   You've got trees in Pilot Street, haven't you?

CAROL   We did have till last bommy night – the kids chopped 'em all down an' burnt them all. *(pause)* Miss, y' know when I grow up, miss. Y' know if I started to work hard now an' learned how to read, eh? Well, d' y' think I'd be able t' live in one of them nice places?

Pause.

MRS KAY   Well you could try, couldn't you, love. Eh?

CAROL   Yeh.

MRS KAY *smiles at her and links her arm. At the back, the* KIDS *are all stifled and bored by* BRIGGS'S *presence.*

BRIGGS   *(Pointing out of the window at the South Docks.)* Now just look at that over there.

DIGGA *looks but sees nothing.*

DIGGA   What?

BRIGGS	What? Can't y' see? Look, those buildings. Don't you ever bother looking at what's around you?
REILLY	It's only the docks, sir.
BRIGGS	You don't get buildings like that anymore. Just look at the work that must have gone into that.
REILLY	D' you like it down here, sir?
BRIGGS	I'm often down here at weekends, taking notes, photographs. (*sharply*) Are you listening, Reilly? There's a wealth of history that won't be here much longer.
REILLY	Me old man works down here, sir.
BRIGGS	What does he think about it?
REILLY	He hates it.
BRIGGS	His job or the place?
REILLY	The whole lot.
BRIGGS	Well, you tell him to stop and have a look at what's around him. Yes, he might see things a bit differently then.

BRIGGS *looks up and sees* LINDA *kneeling up on her seat and talking to the girl behind her.*

KAREN	Wales is cracker.
BRIGGS	Linda Croxley!
LINDA	(*not even looking up*) What?

BRIGGS *gets up and goes across to her. She waits until the last possible moment before sitting 'properly' in her seat.*

BRIGGS	What sort of outfit's that for a school visit?

She is dressed in the prevailing pop outfit of the day.

LINDA	(*Chewing. Contemptuous. Looking out of window.*) What!
BRIGGS	Don't you 'what' me young lady.

(*She shrugs.*)

You know very well that on school visits you wear

school uniform.

LINDA   Well. Mrs Kay never said nott'n about it.

BRIGGS   You're not talking to Mrs Kay.

LINDA   Yeh. I know.

           Pause.

BRIGGS   (*Leaning in close. Threatening.*) Now listen here
           young lady – I don't like your attitude one bit!

LINDA   What have I said? I haven't said nott'n yet, have I?

BRIGGS   I'm talking about your attitude. (pause) I'm telling
           you now. Carry on like this and you'll be spending
           your time in Conwy inside this coach.

LINDA   I don't care. I don't wanna see no crappy castle
           anyway.

BRIGGS   (*pointing*) Count yourself lucky you're not a lad.
           (*pause*) Now I'm warning you, Miss Croxley, cause
           any more unpleasantness on this trip and I'll see to
           it that it's the last you ever go on. (*pause*) Is that
           understood? Is it?

LINDA   (*still looking out of window*) Yes.

           She sighs.

BRIGGS   It better had be.

           (*He makes his way down to the front of the coach
           and takes his seat next to* ANDREWS. *Across the aisle*
           BRIGGS *sees that* MRS KAY *has taken off her shoes and
           has her stockinged feet curled up under her.* CAROL
           has her arm linked through MRS KAY*'s and is
           snuggled up to her – they look more like mother and
           daughter than teacher and pupil. Behind* BRIGGS,
           LINDA *is kneeling up again,* REILLY *and company have
           started smoking and there are lots of* KIDS *eating
           sweets, drinking lemonade and larking about. He
           addresses the* KID *next to* ANDREWS.)

           Right, what's your name? (*pause*) Wake up!

MAURICE   Sir, me!

BRIGGS	What's your name?
MAURICE	McNally, sir.
BRIGGS	Right, McNally, go and sit at the back.
MAURICE	Sir, what for?
BRIGGS	Never mind what for, just do what you're told, lad.

(MAURICE *goes to the back of the coach.* BRIGGS *addresses* ANDREWS.) Right, move up! How long have you been smoking, Andrews?

ANDREWS	Sir, I don't smoke.

(*pause as* BRIGGS *looks at him*)

Sir, since I was eight, sir.

BRIGGS	And how old are you now?
ANDREWS	Sir, thirteen, sir.
BRIGGS	What do your parents say about it?
ANDREWS	Sir, sir, me mum says nott'n about it but when me dad comes home, sir, sir, he belts me.
BRIGGS	Because you smoke?
ANDREWS	Sir, no sir, because I won't give him one.

Pause.

BRIGGS	Your father goes to sea does he?
ANDREWS	What? No, sir.
BRIGGS	You said 'when he comes home', I thought you meant he was away a lot.
ANDREWS	He is, sir, but he doesn't go to sea.
BRIGGS	What does he do?
ANDREWS	I dunno, sir, sir, he just comes round every now an' then an' has a barney with me mam. Then he goes off again. I think he tries to get money off her but she won't give him it though. She hates him. We all hate him.

Pause.

BRIGGS	Listen. Why don't you promise yourself that you'll

give up smoking. You must realise it's bad for your health.

ANDREWS Sir, I do, sir. I've got a terrible cough.

BRIGGS Well, why don't you pack it in?

ANDREWS Sir, sir, I can't.

BRIGGS Thirteen and you can't stop smoking!

ANDREWS No, sir.

BRIGGS (*sighing, shaking his head*) Well you'd better not let me catch you again.

ANDREWS No, sir, I won't.

Pause as they each go into their respective thoughts. BRIGGS *turns and looks at* MRS KAY. *She looks at him and smiles warmly. He tries to respond but doesn't quite make it.* COLIN *walks along the aisle generally checking that everything is all right. As he gets near* LINDA*'s seat her friend,* KAREN, *taps her and points him out.* LINDA *immediately turns round and smiles at* COLIN. *It's obvious that she fancies him.*

LINDA Sir, y' comin' to sit by me are y'?

KAREN (*on the seat behind* LINDA) Don't sit by her, sir … come an' sit by me.

COLIN I've got a seat at the front, thanks.

LINDA 'Ey, sir.

COLIN What, Linda?

LINDA Come here, I wanna tell y' somethin'.

COLIN Well, go on.

LINDA Ah ey sir, I don't want everyone to hear. Come on, just sit down here while I tell y'.

KAREN Come on, sir … she won't harm y'.

LINDA Come on, sir.

Reluctantly COLIN *sits by her.* KAREN'S *head is poking through the space between the seats and both girls laugh.*

COLIN	What is it?

(*They laugh.*)

You're not goin' to tell me a joke, are you?

(*The girls laugh even more.*)

Well, I'll have to go.

LINDA *quickly links her arm through his and holds him there.*

LINDA No, sir ... listen. Listen, she said, I wouldn't tell y' ... but I will. (*pause*) Sir, I think you're lovely.

COLIN (*Quickly getting up. Embarrassed.*) Linda!

He walks away from the girls to the back of the coach.

LINDA I told him. I said I would. Ooh ... he's ace isn't he?

KAREN You've got no chance. He's goin' with miss.

LINDA I know. (*pause*) He might chuck her though an' start goin' with me. He might marry me.

KAREN (*shrieking*) Ooer! Don't be stupid, you. You won't get a husband like sir. You'll end up marryin' someone like your old feller.

LINDA You're just jealous you, girl.

KAREN Get lost.

COLIN *talks to the lads on the back seat.* REILLY *hides a cigarette in his cupped hand.*

COLIN All right lads ... it shouldn't be too long before we're getting into Wales.

LITTLE KID That's in the country, Wales, isn't it, sir?

COLIN A lot of it is countryside, yes.

REILLY Lots of woods, eh sir?

COLIN Woods and mountains, lakes ...

REILLY You gonna take miss into the woods, are y', sir?

COLIN (*pause*) Now just watch it, Brian, all right?

REILLY Sir, I just meant was y' gonna show her the trees an' the plants ...

COLIN I know quite well what you meant.

(*turns to go*)

And if I was you I'd put that fag out before you burn your hand. If Mr Briggs sees that you'll be spending the rest of the day alongside him. Now come on, put it out.

REILLY *takes a last mammoth drag and then stubs out the cigarette.* COLIN *walks back along the aisle.*

REILLY (*Shouting after him.*) I'll show her the woods for y', sir.

(COLIN *pretends not to hear.* REILLY *leans across to the* LITTLE KID *in the seat in front and knocks him.*)

Give us a sweet you, greedy guts.

LITTLE KID I've only a few left.

DIGGA You've got loads.

LITTLE KID I haven't.

REILLY Let's have a look then.

(*The* LITTLE KID *falls for it and shows him the bag.* REILLY *snatches it.*)

Ta!

SCENE SEVEN **IN THE COUNTRY**

The coach is on a country road. MRS KAY *is talking to the* DRIVER.

MRS KAY Ronny, I was just wondering, is there somewhere round here we could stop and let the kids stretch their legs a bit?

DRIVER Well I'll tell y' what, Mrs Kay, there's a few cafés a bit further on. D' y' want me to pull into one of them?

MRS KAY Smashing.

SCENE EIGHT **A ROADSIDE CAFÉ**

Outside the café there are signs saying: 'Open' and 'Coaches Welcome'. Inside the café, a WAITRESS *is working on the tables. There is also a woman,* MRS ROBERTS, *working behind the counter.*

WAITRESS (*Looking up and seeing coach in distance.*) Better be getting some cups ready, Mrs Roberts. There's a coach comin'.

MRS ROBERTS (*Moving over to window.*) Where is it?

WAITRESS Probably pensioners so early in the season.

MRS ROBERTS (*worried*) No. I don't ... I don't think so.

(She moves behind the counter and produces a pair of binoculars.)

Let me see.

(She lifts the binoculars and looks at the coach. She can see the KIDS *and the destination indicator which reads: 'Liverpool to Conwy'. She lowers the binoculars and frowns a worried frown.)*

Right! Come on, action!

SCENE NINE **INSIDE THE COACH**

MR BRIGGS *is addressing the* KIDS.

BRIGGS Now the folk who run these places provide a good and valuable service to travellers like us ... so remember what I've said.

SCENE TEN **BACK AT THE CAFÉ**

The café is alive with activity: the shutters are coming down, the 'Coaches Welcome' sign is replaced by 'Absolutely no Coaches' and the 'Open' sign by one saying 'Closed'. The doors are locked and bolted; MRS ROBERTS *and the* WAITRESS *lean against the door.*

SCENE ELEVEN **IN THE COACH**

The coach has pulled up. The DRIVER *and* MRS KAY *are looking at the café.*

MRS KAY   Perhaps it's because it's so early in the season. Maybe if they knew there was the chance of some business they'd open for us. I'll go and give them a knock.

SCENE TWELVE **IN THE CAFÉ**

Inside, the two women are silent, terrified. They hear footsteps coming up the drive. The door is knocked upon. MRS KAY *is on the other side of the door watched by the* KIDS *from the coach windows. She knocks again.*

MRS ROBERTS   (*from within*) We are closed!

MRS KAY   You couldn't possibly …

MRS ROBERTS   (*firm*) We are closed.

(MRS KAY *moves away. As the two women hear the receding footsteps, they sigh.*)

I only ever did it once, take a Liverpool coach load. I tell you not one word of a lie Miss Powell, they'd rob your eyes if you wasn't lookin'.

The coach pulls away. The KIDS *give V-signs to the café and cross their legs to stop themselves from wetting.*

SCENE THIRTEEN **A CAFÉ AND SHOP**

On the window a sign reads: 'Under New Management'. Inside, two men, JOHN *and* MAC, *are behind the counter generally preparing their place for the season.*

JOHN   Look, how many times, listen, it's only the start of the season innit? Eh? Course it is. We can't make a bloody fortune before the season's begun, can we?

    MAC See, it's no that what's worryin' me. What I think, see, is we bought the wrong place. If you was askin' me, I'd say the coaches'll stop at the first café they come to. An' that's up the road.

    JOHN Some of them will, yeh. But there'll be enough for us as well. Give it a month, that's all; y' won't be able t' see this road for coaches. Thousands of schoolkids with money t' burn. We'll clean up, mate.

    (*They hear the sound of brakes and of tyres pulling up.* JOHN *looks out of the window.*)

    Now what did I say, eh?

    MAC (*Looking out of window. Brightening.*) Look at that. Christ, there's hundreds of them.

    JOHN Right. Let's go. Come on.

    He moves to the counter and points out the items quickly.

    JOHN Jelly Babies: fifteen p. a quarter.

    MAC I thought they was only twelve.

    JOHN Ice creams nine p.

    MAC They was only seven p. yesterday.

    JOHN Listen, mate, can I help inflation?

    MAC (*Getting the picture.*) Oh right. I get the picture.

    JOHN Passin' trade mate. Always soak the passin' trade. Y' never see them again so it don't matter. Bubble Gum two p. – no, make that three. Ice lollies ten p. Come on … get those doors open. We'll milk this little lot.

SCENE FOURTEEN **IN THE CAR PARK**

The KIDS *are tumbling off the coach.* MRS KAY *takes out a flask and sits on a bench in the café garden.* BRIGGS *is frantic.*

    BRIGGS Stop! Slater, walk … walk! You, boy … come here. Now stop. All of you … stop!

MRS KAY   (*pouring out coffee*) Mr Briggs, they'll …

BRIGGS   (*To a boy,* RONSON, *who is rushing for the door of the shop.*) Ronson! Come here!

RONSON *stops and walks back to* BRIGGS, *shrugging.*

MRS KAY   Mr Briggs … as long as they don't go near the road I don't think there's any …

BRIGGS   All right, Mrs Kay.

(RONSON *stands in front of him.*)

Now just where do you think you are?

(RONSON *is puzzled.*)

Well?

RONSON *looks round for help in answering. There is none.*

RONSON   (*sincerely*) Sir, Wales?

SCENE FIFTEEN **INSIDE THE SHOP**

The counter cannot be seen for pushing, impatient KIDS. *The two men are working frantically as orders are fired at them from all quarters. As the orders are shouted, the* KIDS *are robbing stuff left, right and centre – it's the usual trick but the two men are falling for it – the* KIDS *point to jars high up, as the men turn their backs, so racks of chocolate bars disappear into eager pockets.*

SCENE SIXTEEN **OUTSIDE THE SHOP**

BRIGGS   And don't let me catch you at it again. Now go on. Walk.

(*He watches as* RONSON *walks into the shop. Satisfied, he turns to* MRS KAY.)

Now, Mrs Kay, what was it you wanted?

MRS KAY   Well, I just thought you might like to have a sit down away from them for a few minutes.

BRIGGS   To be quite honest, Mrs Kay I think we should all be inside, looking after them. Do you think it was wise just letting them all pour in there at once?

MRS KAY   Ooh ... leave them. They've been cooped up for over an hour. They'll want to stretch their legs and let off a bit of steam.

BRIGGS   I don't mind them stretching their legs. It's not the children I'm concerned about.

MRS KAY   Well, just who are you concerned about?

BRIGGS   There's not only our school to think about, you know. There's others who come after us and they're dependent upon the goodwill of the people who run these places.

MRS KAY   (*pouring out another cup of coffee*) Considering the profit they make out of the kids I don't think they've got much to complain about.

BRIGGS   (*taking cup*) Thanks. (*pause*) You know, I'll have to say this to you, Mrs Kay, there are times when I really think you're on their side.

    Pause.

MRS KAY   And I'll have to say this to you, Mr Briggs, I didn't ask you to come on this trip.

BRIGGS   No, but the Headmaster did.

SCENE SEVENTEEN **OUTSIDE THE COACH**

The last few stragglers climb on board.

MRS KAY   (*to the* KIDS) Are you the last? Anyone left in the toilet?

SUSAN   (*As she finishes counting heads.*) That's the lot. We've got them all.

MRS KAY   All right Ron.

DRIVER   Right love.

    He starts the engine.

SCENE EIGHTEEN **IN THE SHOP**

The KIDS *have gone and the shelves are almost bare.*
The two men sit back, exhausted but satisfied.

MAC If I hadn't seen it with m' own eyes.

JOHN I told y'.

MAC We'll have to re-order.

JOHN An' that's just one coachload.

MAC We must've took a bloody fortune.

JOHN There was sixty quid's worth of stock on those shelves an' most of it's gone.

MAC Come ... let's count up.

(He gets up, goes to the till and opens it. It contains a lot of change but hardly any notes. He is puzzled.)

Was you lookin' after the notes?

JOHN Which notes? I thought you was takin' care of them.

MAC Well, we must of taken a load of notes.

He looks at the bare shelves.

SCENE NINETEEN **INSIDE THE COACH**

The KIDS *are weighed down with sweets.*

SCENE TWENTY **THE SHOP**

MAC The thievin' little bastards!

He rushes for the door. JOHN *follows. As he flings back the door he sees the coach just pulling away down the road. They run after the disappearing coach. The back window is a mass of two-fingered gestures. The two men are finally left standing in the road.*

SCENE TWENTY-ONE **IN THE COACH**

MRS KAY *leaves her seat and goes over to* SUSAN*'s seat.* SUSAN *is playing 'I Spy' with a couple of girls who are sitting with her.* BRIGGS *moves across to talk to* COLIN. *He is conspiratorial.*

BRIGGS   You know what her problem is, don't you?

COLIN   (*Trying to keep out of it. Looking out of window.*) Mm?

BRIGGS   Well, she thinks I can't see through all this woolly-headed liberalism, you know what I mean? I mean, all right, she has her methods, I have mine but I can't see why she has to set herself up as the great champion of the non-academics. Can you? It might look like love and kindness but if you ask me I don't think it does the kids a scrap of good.

COLIN   Erm ... .

BRIGGS   I mean, I think you have to risk being disliked if you're going to do any good for these type of kids. They've got enough freedom at home, haven't they, with their two quid pocket money and television till all hours, haven't they? (*pause*) I don't know what you think but I think her philosophy is totally confused. What do you think?

BRIGGS *waits for an answer.*

COLIN   Actually, I don't think it's got anything to do with a philosophy.

BRIGGS   What? You mean you haven't noticed all this, sort of, anti-establishment, let the kids roam wild, don't check them attitude?

COLIN   Of course I've noticed it. But she's like that all the time. This trip isn't organised according to any startling theory.

BRIGGS   Well what is the method she works to then? I mean, you tell me, you know her better than I do.

COLIN   The only principle behind today is that the kids should have a good day out.

BRIGGS   Well that's all I'm saying, but if they're going to have a good and stimulating day then it's got to be planned and executed better than this.

(*While* BRIGGS *is talking,* MRS KAY *has moved to have a word with the* DRIVER. *Suddenly the coach swings into a driveway.* BRIGGS *is startled and puzzled.*)

What's this ... where are we ...

MRS KAY   It's all right, Mr Briggs ... I've checked it with the Driver. I thought it would be a good idea if we called into the zoo for an hour. We've got plenty of time.

BRIGGS   But I thought this trip was organised so that the kids could see Conwy Castle.

MRS KAY   We'll be going to the castle after. (*to the* KIDS) Now listen, everybody. As a sort of extra bonus, we've decided to call in here and let you have an hour at the zoo.

Cheers.

BRIGGS   Look, we can't ... .

MRS KAY   Now the rest of the staff and myself will be around if you want to know anything about the animals – mind you, there's not much point in asking me, because I don't know one monkey from the next.

REILLY   (*shouting from the back*) Apart from Andrews, miss, he's a gorilla.

ANDREWS *gives him a V-sign.*

MRS KAY   And yourself, Brian, the Orang Utang.

The KIDS *laugh.* REILLY *waves his fist.*

DIGGA   Don't worry, miss, he's a big baboon.

MRS KAY   Now let's not have any silly name-calling.

BRIGGS   (*whispering in* MRS KAY*'s ear*) Mrs Kay ...

MRS KAY   (*ignoring him*) Now as I was saying, I don't know a great deal about the animals but we're very lucky to have Mr Briggs with us because he's something of an expert in natural history. So, if any of you want to know more about the animals you see, Mr Briggs will tell you all about them. Come on, leave your things on the coach.

KID Agh, great.

The KIDS *begin to get up.*

SCENE TWENTY-TWO **THE ZOO**

The KIDS *wander around in groups – pulling faces at the animals, pointing and running, girls walking arm in arm. They point and shriek with horrified delight at the sexual organs of monkeys.* MR BRIGGS *is with a group of* KIDS *looking at a large bear in a pit.*

BRIGGS ... and so you can see with those claws it could give you a very nasty mark.

ANDREWS An' could it kill y', sir?

BRIGGS Well, why do you think it's kept in a pit?

RONSON I think that's cruel. Don't you?

BRIGGS No. Not if it's treated well. And don't forget it was born in captivity so it won't know any other sort of life.

RONSON I'll bet it does, sir.

GIRL 1 How do you know? Sir's just told y' hasn't he? If it was born in a cage an' it's lived all its life in a pit, well, it won't know nothin' else so it won't want nothin' else, will it?

RONSON Well, why does it kill people then?

ANDREWS What's that got to do with it?

RONSON It kills them cos they're cruel to it. They keep it in a pit so when it gets out it's bound to be mad an' wanna kill people. Don't you see?

ANDREWS Sir, he's thick. Tell him to shurrup, sir.

RONSON	I'm not thick. If it lived there all its life it must know, mustn't it, sir?
BRIGGS	Know what?
ANDREWS	Sir, he's nuts.
RONSON	It must know about other ways of living, sir. Y' know, free, like the way people have stopped it livin'. It only kills people cos it's trapped an' people are always stood lookin' at it. If it was free it wouldn't bother people at all.
BRIGGS	Well, I wouldn't be so sure about that, Ronson.
ANDREWS	Sir's right. Bears kill y' cos it's in them t' kill y'.
GIRL 2	Agh come on, sir … let's go to the Children's Zoo.
ANDREWS	Let's go to the big ones.
BRIGGS	It's all right … we'll get round them all eventually.
GIRL 1	Sir, we goin' the Children's Zoo then.
BRIGGS	If you want to.
GIRL 1	Come on.

BRIGGS *starts to walk away. The two girls link his arms, one either side. He stops.*

BRIGGS	Oh! (*taking their arms away*) Walk properly.
GIRL 2	Agh ey, sir, the other teachers let y' link them.

MRS KAY *is with another group. She sees* BRIGGS.

MRS KAY	Oh hello. How are you getting on? They plying you with questions?
BRIGGS	Yes, they've been very good.
MRS KAY	I'm just going for a cup of coffee. Do you want to join me?
BRIGGS	Well I was just on my way to the Children's Zoo with these.
ANDREWS	It's all right, sir. We'll go on our own.
MRS KAY	Oh come on. They'll be all right.
BRIGGS	Well, I don't know if these people can be trusted on their own, Mrs Kay.

MRS KAY It's all right, Susan and Colin are walking round and the place is walled in. They'll be all right.

ANDREWS Go on, sir. You go an' get a cuppa. Y' can trust us.

BRIGGS Ah! Can I though? If I go off for a cup of coffee with Mrs Kay can you people be trusted to act responsibly?

Chorus of 'Yes, sir'.

BRIGGS All right Mrs Kay. We'll trust them to act responsibly.

MRS KAY Come on.

They walk off to the zoo café.

SCENE TWENTY-THREE **THE BIRD HOUSE**

Two boys are slowly repeating, 'Everton, Everton' to two blue and yellow macaws.

BOY Go on, just tweek it out, you dislocated sparrow … speak!

SCENE TWENTY-FOUR **THE CHILDREN'S ZOO**

The KIDS *watch a collection of small animals – rabbits, gerbils, guinea-pigs, bantam hens – all contained in an open pit.* RONSON *looks fondly at a rabbit.*

RONSON They're great, aren't they?

CAROL They're lovely.

RONSON (*Bending over and stroking a rabbit.*) Come on … come on …

CAROL 'Ey you. Y' not supposed t' touch them.

(RONSON *answers by picking up the rabbit and gently stroking it.* CAROL *reaches over to join him stroking the rabbit but he pulls it close to him protectively.*)

Well. I'll get one of me own.

(*She bends down and picks up a guinea-pig which she strokes affectionately.*)

These are better anyway!

SCENE TWENTY-FIVE **THE ZOO CAFÉ**

MR BRIGGS *and* MRS KAY *are waiting for coffee at the service rail.*

BRIGGS   How many sugars, Mrs Kay?

MRS KAY   Call me Helen. I hate being called Mrs Kay all the time. Makes me feel old. I tried to get the kids to call me Helen once. I had the class full of them chanting it. Two minutes later they were calling me Mrs Kay again. No, no sugar, thank you.

SCENE TWENTY-SIX **THE CHILDREN'S ZOO**

More KIDS *have followed* RONSON *'s example. Quite a few of them are now clutching furry friends.*

CAROL   I'm gonna call mine Freddy. Hiya, Freddy. Hello, Freddy. Freddy.

SCENE TWENTY-SEVEN **THE ZOO CAFÉ**

MRS KAY *and* BRIGGS *are sitting at a table; she lights a cigarette.*

BRIGGS   They're really interested, you know, really interested in the animals.

MRS KAY   I thought they'd enjoy it here.

BRIGGS   Perhaps when we're back in school we could arrange something; maybe I could come along and give them a small talk with some slides that I've got.

MRS KAY   (*enthusiastically*) Oh, would you?

BRIGGS   You should have asked me to do something a long time ago.

MRS KAY   Well, don't forget you've never offered before.

BRIGGS   To tell you the truth I didn't think the kids who came to you would be too interested in animals.

SCENE TWENTY-EIGHT **THE CHILDREN'S ZOO**

The animal pit is empty. The children have gone.

SCENE TWENTY-NINE **THE COACH**

BRIGGS *and* MRS KAY *approach.*

BRIGGS   Don't worry, we'll get that arranged as soon as we get back to school.

SUSAN *and* COLIN *stand by the coach with the* DRIVER.

COLIN   (*to* DRIVER) You should have come round with us, it's a grand zoo.

DRIVER   A couple of hours kip – seen it all before.

COLIN   You'd have had a good time.

MRS KAY   All on board?

SUSAN   Yes. We wandered back and most of them were already here.

MRS KAY   Oh! That makes a change.

BRIGGS   All checked and present. Right. Off we go.

The DRIVER *and the* TEACHERS *climb on board. In the distance the* ANIMAL KEEPER, *polo-necked and wellied, runs towards the coach. Inside the coach the* KIDS *sit like angels. The coach pulls away but the* ANIMAL KEEPER *waves it down. It stops. The* KEEPER *strides on board.*

MRS KAY   Have we forgotten something?

KEEPER   Are you supposed to be in charge of this lot?

MRS KAY   Why? What's the matter?

KEEPER   Children. They're not bloody children. They're

animals. That's not a zoo out there. This is the
bloody zoo, in here!

BRIGGS   Would you mind controlling your language and
telling me what's going on.

KEEPER   (*Ignoring him and pushing past him to the* KIDS.)
Right. Come on. Where are they?

(*The* KIDS *look back innocently.*)

Call yourselves teachers. You can't even control
them.

BRIGGS   Now look. This has just gone far enough. Would
you tell me exactly what you want please?

A clucking hen is heard. The KEEPER *turns and looks.
A* KID *is fidgeting with his coat. The* KEEPER *strides up
to him and pulls back his coat, revealing a bantam
hen. Two more* KEEPERS *come on board. The first*
KEEPER *grabs the hen and addresses the* KIDS.

KEEPER   Right! And now I want the rest!

*There is a moment's hesitation before the floodgates
are opened. Animals appear from every conceivable
hiding-place. The coach becomes a menagerie.* MRS
KAY *raises her eyebrows to heaven. The* KEEPERS *collect
the animals.* BRIGGS *stares icily.*

SCENE THIRTY **THE COACH, MOMENTS LATER**

BRIGGS *is outside talking to the* KEEPERS, *who have
collected all the animals in small cages. They walk
away and* BRIGGS *climbs on to the coach. His face is
like thunder. The* KIDS *try to look anywhere but at him
– trying to avoid the unavoidable.* BRIGGS *pauses for a
long, staring, angry and contemptuous moment.*

BRIGGS   I trusted you lot. (*pause*) I trusted you. And this, is
the way you repay me. (*pause*) I trusted all of you,
but it's obvious that trust is something you know
nothing about.

RONSON   Sir, we only borrowed them.

BRIGGS   (*shouting*) Shut up, lad! (*pause*) Is it any wonder
that people won't do anything for you? The minute
we start to treat you as real people, what happens?
That man was right, you act like animals, animals!
(*pause*) Well I've learned a lesson today. Oh, yes, I
have. I've learned that trust is something you people
don't understand. Now, I'm warning you, all of you,
don't expect any more trust from me!

(*The* KIDS *are resigned. They have heard it all before.*
BRIGGS *turns to* MRS KAY.)

Mrs Kay. When we get to the castle we'll split up
into four groups. Each member of staff will be
responsible for one group.

MRS KAY *looks at him.*

SCENE THIRTY-ONE **CONWY CASTLE**

BRIGGS, *with a group of ordered children standing
behind him, points to a spot high up on the castle.
The* KIDS *all look up, bored.*

BRIGGS   Now you see these larger square holes, just below
the battlements there – well, they were used for …
long planks of wood which supported a sort of
platform, and that's where the archers used to stand
and fire down on the attackers of the castle. Now
what's interesting is, if you look at the side of that
tower it's not quite perpendicular. What's
perpendicular mean?

MILTON   Sir, sir.

BRIGGS   All right, Milton.

MILTON   Straight up, sir. (*Sniggers from the other boys.*)

In another part of the castle, KIDS *are rushing about
playing medieval cowboys and Indians.* MRS KAY *sits
on a bench overlooking the estuary.* CAROL *and*

ANDREWS *are with her. In a secluded passage of the castle,* REILLY *and* DIGGA *are smoking; they are concealed in an alcove.* COLIN'S *voice can be heard. He approaches,* KAREN *and* LINDA *follow close behind him.*

COLIN So, although these walls are nearly fifteen feet thick in places, you still have the wind blasting in through the arrow slits and with no proper heat, you can imagine just how cold it must have been.

LINDA Sir, I wonder what they did to keep warm in the olden days?

COLIN (*stopping and turning*) Well, obviously they ... Where's everybody else gone? Where are the others?

KAREN Sir, they kept dropping out as you were talkin'.

COLIN Oh God.

LINDA It's all right, sir. Y' can keep showin' us round. We're dead interested.

COLIN (*sighing*) All right Linda ... what was I saying?

LINDA Sir, y' was tellin' us how they kept warm in the olden days.

COLIN (*continuing down the passage*) They wore much thicker clothing ... All right, Linda?

LINDA Sir, it's dead spooky. It's haunted isn't it?

COLIN Don't be silly.

LINDA Sir, I'm frightened (*linking his arm for protection*).

COLIN Now, don't do that, Linda!

LINDA (*holding on*) But I'm frightened, sir.

KAREN (*grabbing his other arm*) Sir, so am I.

COLIN (*firmly, freeing himself*) Now, girls, stop being silly. Stop it. There's nothing to be frightened of! Now, come on.

He leads them along the passage. As they pass the alcove where REILLY *and* DIGGA *are concealed,* REILLY *leans out and just gently touches* LINDA *'s shoulder. She screams and flings herself at* COLIN, KAREN *reacts and does the same. Even* COLIN *is slightly startled.*

LINDA Sir, it touched me.

COLIN What did?

LINDA Oh, it did.

> COLIN *looks worried. They hear laughter. Just at the point when the three of them are about to run,* REILLY *and* DIGGA *fall laughing out of the alcove. In the distance* BRIGGS *shouts, 'Reilly!'* REILLY *and* DIGGA *hear him and leg away past* COLIN *and the terrified girls. Outside,* MRS KAY, CAROL *and* ANDREWS *still sit looking out over the estuary.*

MRS KAY Why don't you go and have a look around the castle grounds. You haven't seen it yet.

CAROL Miss, I don't like it. It's horrible. I just like sittin' here with you, lookin' at the lake.

MRS KAY That's not a lake, love. It's the sea.

CAROL That's what I meant, miss.

ANDREWS Miss, wouldn't it be great if we had something like this round ours. Then the kids wouldn't get into trouble if they had somewhere like this to play, would they?

CAROL Miss. Couldn't have nothin' like this round our way could they?

MRS KAY Why not?

CAROL Cos we'd only wreck it, wouldn't we?

ANDREWS No, we wouldn't.

CAROL We would, y' know. That's why we never have nothin' nice round our way – cos we'd just smash it up. The Corpy knows that so why should they waste their money, eh? They'd give us things if we looked after them, but we don't look after them, do we?

ANDREWS Miss, miss, y' know what I think about it, eh, miss.

MRS KAY Go on, John. What do you think?

ANDREWS   Miss, if all this belonged to us, miss, and it was ours, not the Corpy's but, ours, well, we wouldn't let no one wreck it would we? We'd defend it.

BRIGGS *approaches, obviously angry.*

BRIGGS   You two … off! Go on. Move.

CAROL   Sir, where?

BRIGGS   Anywhere, girl. Just move. I want to speak to Mrs Kay. Well, come on then.

The two kids, CAROL *and* ANDREWS, *wander off.* BRIGGS *waits until they are out of hearing range.*

MRS KAY   I was talking to those children.

BRIGGS   Yes, and I'm talking to you, Mrs Kay. It's got to stop, this has.

MRS KAY   What has?

BRIGGS   What has? Can't y' see what's goin' on? It's a shambles, the whole ill-organised affair. Look at what they did at the zoo. Just look at them here.

(*All around the castle they can see, from where they sit,* KIDS *running, pulling, laughing and shouting.*)

They're just left to race and chase and play havoc. God knows what the castle authorities must think. Look, when you bring children like ours into this sort of environment you can't afford to just let them go free. They're just like town dogs let off the lead in the country. My God, for some of them it's the first time they've been further than Birkenhead.

MRS KAY   (*quietly*) I know. And I was just thinking; it's a shame really, isn't it, eh? You know, we bring them to a crumbling pile of bricks and mortar and they think they're in the fields of heaven.

Pause. He glares at her.

BRIGGS   (*accusing*) You *are* on their side aren't you?

MRS KAY   (*looking at him*) Absolutely, Mr Briggs. Absolutely!

BRIGGS   Look! All I want to know from you is what you're

going to do about this chaos.

MRS KAY Well, I'd suggest that if you want the chaos to stop, then you should stop seeing it as chaos. All right, the Headmaster asked you to come along – but can't you relax? There's no point in pretending that a day out to Wales is going to furnish them with the education they should have had long ago. It's too late for them. Most of them were rejects on the day they were born, Mr Briggs. We're not going to solve anything today. Can't we just try and give them a good day out? At least we could try and do that.

BRIGGS (*the castle looming behind him*) Well, that's a fine attitude isn't it? That's a fine attitude for a member of the teaching profession to have.

MRS KAY (*Beginning to lose her temper ever so slightly.*) Well, what's your alternative? Eh? Do you really think there's any point pretending? Even if you cared do you think you could educate these kids, my remedial kids? Because you're a fool if you do. You won't educate them because nobody wants them educating …

BRIGGS Listen Mrs Kay …

MRS KAY No, you listen, Mr Briggs, you listen and perhaps you'll stop fooling yourself. Teach them? Teach them what? You'll never teach them because nobody knows what to do with them. Ten years ago you could teach them to stand in a line, you could teach them to obey, to expect little more than a lousy factory job. But now they haven't even got that to aim for. Mr Briggs, you won't teach them because you're in a job that's designed and funded to fail! There's nothing for them to do, any of them; most of them were born for factory fodder, but the factories have closed down.

BRIGGS And I suppose that's the sort of stuff you've been pumping into their minds, is it?

MRS KAY (*laughing*) And you really think they'd understand?

BRIGGS   Listen, I'm not going to spend any more time
arguing with you. You may have organised this
visit, but I'm the one who's been sent by the
Headmaster to supervise. Now, either you take
control of the children in your charge or I'll be
forced to abandon this visit and order everyone
home.

Pause. She looks at him.

MRS KAY   Well ... that's your decision. But I'm not going to let
you prevent the kids from having some fun. If you
want to abandon this visit then you'd better start
walking because we're not going home. We're
going to the beach.

BRIGGS   The beach!!

MRS KAY   We can't come all the way to the seaside and not go
down to the beach!

She turns and walks away.

SCENE THIRTY-TWO **THE BEACH**

BRIGGS *sits on a rock apart from the main group.* MRS
KAY *is paddling, dress held above her knees looking
old-fashioned, with a group of* KIDS. *Girls are
screaming in delight and boys are laughing and
running. Two boys,* KEVIN *and* JIMMY, *are near* MRS
KAY.

JIMMY   'Ey, miss, we could have brought our costumes an'
gone swimmin'.

KEVIN   We could go swimmin' anyway, couldn't we, miss?

CAROL   (*Trailing behind* MRS KAY.) Miss, when do we have
to go home?

JIMMY   What? In your undies?

KEVIN   Yeh. Why not?

MRS KAY   No. Not today.

KEVIN   Agh ... why not, miss.

MRS KAY Because …

JIMMY If y' went swimmin' in just y' undies, the police would pick y' up, wouldn't they, miss?

MRS KAY Look, the reason I don't want you to go swimming is because there aren't enough staff here to guarantee that it would be safe. I want to go home with a full coachload thank you.

CAROL Miss, when d' we have t' go …

KEVIN Agh, miss, I'd be all right, miss … I wouldn't get drowned, miss.

MRS KAY (*warning*) Kevin!

KEVIN Oh, miss.

MRS KAY Kevin, I've already explained why I don't want you to go swimming …

KEVIN Oh … Miss …

MRS KAY Carry on like that and I'll have to sort you out.

KEVIN Agh …

She stops him with a warning look. He tuts. Satisfied that he won't take it any further, she turns to CAROL.

MRS KAY Right …

KEVIN Just for five minutes, miss.

MRS KAY (*Turning and walking towards him.*) Kevin Bryant … come here.

KEVIN (*Backing away. Laughing.*) Ah, miss, I didn't mean it … honest miss. I never meant it.

(MRS KAY, *glaring in mock seriousness, comes after him. He is laughing. He breaks and runs. She chases him, skirts trailing in the water, with the other* KIDS *shouting and jeering and urging her to catch him.* KEVIN *is hardly able to run because of laughing so much.* MRS KAY *charges on through the water, looking incongruous.* KEVIN *suddenly stops, turns, bends down in the water and prepares to send up a spray.*)

Don't, miss … don't or I'll spray y'.

MRS KAY Kevin Bryant … you'll do what? … You wait till I get hold of you.

They face each other. The KIDS *at the water's edge chant and shout: 'Get him, Miss', 'Duck him, Miss', 'Throw him in', 'Y've had it now, Bryant'.* KEVIN *makes the mistake of turning to the group of* KIDS *to answer them. In a flash she is on him and turns him upside-down. She ducks him and he comes up spluttering and laughing. The other* KIDS *cheer and laugh.*

KEVIN Oh no, miss.

MRS KAY Now who wanted to go swimming, Kevin?

KEVIN Oh miss, miss. Me 'air's all wet.

(*She quickly lifts him so that she is carrying him, cradle fashion, out of the water.* BRIGGS *looks on. He turns away.* MRS KAY *and* KEVIN *walk away from the water. He shakes water from his hair.*)

Miss … I might get a cold though. I hate that.

MRS KAY Oh, you're like an old woman. Come on then.

She reaches in her bag and produces a towel. She wraps the towel round his head and rubs vigorously. Beneath the towel KEVIN *is beaming and happy.*

KEVIN Ta miss.

CAROL (*at the side of* MRS KAY) Miss, when do we have t' go home?

MRS KAY What's the matter, love? Aren't you enjoying it?

CAROL Yeh, but I don't wanna go home. I wanna stay here.

MRS KAY Oh, Carol, love … we're here for at least another hour. Why don't you start enjoying yourself instead of worrying about going home.

CAROL Cos I don't wanna go home, miss.

MRS KAY Carol, love … We have to go home. It can't be like this all the time.

CAROL Why not?

MRS KAY (*She looks at her and sighs.*) I don't know, love.

SCENE THIRTY-THREE **THE ROCKS**

COLIN *and* SUSAN, LINDA *and* KAREN *and some other*
KIDS *are searching among the rocks.* REILLY *and* DIGGA
are nearby with a smaller group of followers. They
are having a smoke behind a large rock.

ANDREWS Gis a drag.

DIGGA Go an' buy some.

ANDREWS Don't be sly, come on.

REILLY *blows smoke in their faces. As they rush for it, he*
drops it and stubs it out in the sand with his foot. The
KIDS *fight for it.* REILLY *turns away and looks out from*
the rock. He shouts across to COLIN *and* SUSAN*'s group.*

REILLY All right, miss.

COLIN *and* SUSAN *look up.*

COLIN (*quietly*) Ah, here we go.

REILLY (*shouting over*) You comin' for a walk with me then,
miss?

COLIN (*Standing and pointing. Shouting.*) Look … I'm
warning you, Reilly.

SUSAN Don't shout.

COLIN I'm just getting sick of him, that's all.

SUSAN Well, why don't you go and have a word with him?

COLIN I don't know. I just can't seem to get through to
friend Brian. For some reason he seems to have it in
for me.

SUSAN I wonder if I could get through to him.

REILLY Come on … what y' scared of?

SUSAN You go back with the others.

COLIN What are you goin' to …

SUSAN Go on.

COLIN *moves off.* SUSAN *walks slowly across to* REILLY.

LINDA Has miss gone t' sort him out, sir?

KAREN He needs sortin' out, doesn't he, sir?

LINDA He's all right really, y' know, sir. Y' know, when he's on his own he's great.

KAREN Ooer … how d' you know?

LINDA Shut up you.

COLIN All right. All right.

REILLY *smiles.* SUSAN *continues to walk slowly, provocatively, determinedly, towards him. As* SUSAN *stares straight at him,* REILLY *smiles bravely.* REILLY *'s smile gradually disappears as she gets closer. She steps straight up to him – almost against him.* REILLY *looks anywhere but at her.*

SUSAN (*deliberately husky*) Well, Brian … I'm here.

REILLY 'Ey, miss.

SUSAN I'm all yours … handsome!

REILLY Don't mess, miss.

SUSAN (*putting her arms around him*) I'm not messing, Big Boy. I'm serious.

(BRIGGS, *in the distance walking along the beach, stops and looks. He sees them then turns and goes back. Meanwhile,* REILLY *squirms.*)

What's wrong?

REILLY I was only havin' a laugh, miss.

Lots of little faces peer at them from around and on top of the surrounding rocks.

SUSAN You mean … don't tell me you weren't being serious, Brian.

REILLY I was only jokin' with y', miss.

SUSAN (*She keeps him pinned to the rock and speaks quietly in his ear.*) Well, you'd better listen to me Brian. (*pause*) You're a handsome lad, but I'd suggest that in future you stay in your own league instead of trying to take on ladies who could break you into little pieces. All right, we'll leave it at that shall we?

REILLY   Yes, miss.

*She pats him gently on the face. She pulls back and
as she begins to walk away the laughter breaks out.*
REILLY *lunges out and the* KIDS *scatter.* SUSAN *turns
and sees this.*

SUSAN   Brian.

(*He looks up and she motions him over. She is now
the teacher again.*)

You know what we were saying about leagues?

REILLY   Yeh.

SUSAN   Well have you ever thought whose league Linda's
in?

REILLY   (*smiling*) Linda Croxley?

(SUSAN *nods.* REILLY *smiles.*)

Agh 'ey miss, she doesn't fancy me. She's nuts about
sir. No one else can get a chance.

SUSAN   I wouldn't be too sure about that.

(*She turns to go.*)

See you.

REILLY   See y', miss.

(*He turns and walks back to his mates. As he appears
they all start laughing and jeering. He stands
smiling and proud.*)

Well! At least I'm not like you ugly gets. (*There is a
pause during which he grows about two feet.*) I …
am handsome!

SCENE THIRTY-FOUR **THE BEACH**

A game of football is in progress. MRS KAY *is in goal.
She makes a clumsy save and the* KIDS *cheer.* BRIGGS
watches from a distance. MRS KAY *leaves the game
and goes to meet* COLIN *and* SUSAN *who are
approaching.*

MRS KAY Wooh … I'm pooped.

ANDREWS (*shouting from game*) Agh, miss, we've not got a goaly now.

MRS KAY (*shouting back*) It's all right, Carol can go in goal for you now.

(*She looks amongst the group.* COLIN *and* SUSAN *look on.*)

Where is she?

SUSAN Who?

MRS KAY Carol. She went to look for you.

COLIN We haven't seen her.

MRS KAY Well, where is she?

(MRS KAY *scans the beach.* CAROL *cannot be seen.* MRS KAY *looks at* SUSAN.)

You haven't seen her at all?

SUSAN *shakes her head.* MRS KAY *looks over the beach again.*)

Oh she couldn't. Could she?

SUSAN Lost?

MRS KAY Don't say it. Perhaps he's seen her.

(*She shouts across.*)

Mr Briggs … Mr Briggs.

BRIGGS *looks up, rises and then comes over to her.*

SUSAN I hope he has seen her.

MRS KAY Yeh. The only trouble is she didn't go that way.

BRIGGS (*approaching*) Is that it? Are we going home now?

MRS KAY Have you seen Carol Chandler in the last half hour?

BRIGGS Look! I thought I'd made it quite plain that I was having nothing more to do with your outing.

MRS KAY Have you seen Carol Chandler?

BRIGGS No. I haven't.

MRS KAY I think she might have wandered off somewhere.

BRIGGS   You mean you've lost her.

MRS KAY   No. I mean she might have wandered off.

BRIGGS   Well, what's that if it's not losing her? All I can say is it's a wonder you haven't lost half a dozen of them.

COLIN   Listen, Briggs, it's about time someone told you what a burke you are.

BRIGGS   And you listen, sonny. Don't you try telling me a word because you haven't even earned the right. Don't worry, when we get back to school, your number's up. As well as hers.

(*He motions to* MRS KAY.)

And you (*to* SUSAN), I saw what was going on between you and Reilly. When we get back, I'll have the lot of you!

MRS KAY   Would you mind postponing your threats until we've found Carol. At the moment I'd say the most important thing is to find the girl.

BRIGGS   Don't you mean *try* and find her?

MRS KAY   Susan ... you keep these lads playing football. We'll split up and look for her.

MRS KAY, COLIN *and* BRIGGS *walk off in separate directions.*

SCENE THIRTY-FIVE **THE CLIFF**

Below the cliff-top, the sea is breaking on rocks in a cave mouth. In the distance, MRS KAY *is shouting 'Carol, Carol', and* COLIN *is searching the far end of the beach.* CAROL *is standing on top of the cliff watching the waves below. She looks out over the sea. Alone on the cliff-top, she is at peace with the warm sun and small breeze upon her – a fleeting moment of tranquility.*

BRIGGS   Carol Chandler!

(BRIGGS *approaches. On seeing her he stops and stands a few yards off.*)

Just come here.

(*She turns and stares at him.*)

Who gave you permission to come up here?

CAROL No one.

Turning, she dismisses him.

BRIGGS I'm talking to you, Carol Chandler.

(*She continues to ignore his presence.*)

Now just listen here, young lady ...

As he goes to move towards her, she turns on him.

CAROL Don't you come near me!

BRIGGS (*Taken aback. Stopping.*) Pardon!

CAROL I don't want you to come near me.

BRIGGS Well, in that case just get yourself moving and let's get down to the beach.

Pause.

CAROL You go. I'm not comin'.

BRIGGS You what?

CAROL Tell Mrs Kay that she can go home without me. I'm stoppin' here ... in Wales.

Pause.

BRIGGS Now just you listen to me – I've had just about enough today, just about enough, and I'm not putting up with a pile of silliness from the likes of you. Now come on ...

He starts to move towards her. She takes a step towards the edge of the cliff.

CAROL Try an' get me an' I'll jump over.

BRIGGS *stops, astounded. There is an angry pause. She continues to ignore him.*

BRIGGS Now come on! I'll not tell you again.

(*He moves forward. Again, she moves nearer to the edge. He stops and they look at each other.*)

I'll give you five seconds. Just five seconds. One ...
two ... three ... four ... I'm warning you, five!

She stares at him blankly. BRIGGS *stares back in
impotent rage.*

CAROL   I've told y' ... I'm not comin' down with y'.

(*pause*)

I'll jump y' know ... I will.

BRIGGS   Just what are you trying to do to me?

CAROL   I've told you. Leave me alone and I won't jump.

(*pause*)

I wanna stay here. Where it's nice.

BRIGGS   Stay here? How could you stay here? What would
you do? Where would you live?

CAROL   I'd be all right.

BRIGGS   Now I've told you ... stop being so silly.

CAROL   (*turning on him*) What do you worry for, eh? Eh?
You don't care, do y'? Do y'?

BRIGGS   What? About you? Listen ... if I didn't care, why am
I here, now, trying to stop you doing something
stupid.

CAROL   Because if I jumped over, you'll get into trouble
when you get back to school. That's why, Briggsy!
So stop goin' on. You hate me.

BRIGGS   Don't be ridiculous – just because I'm a school
teacher it doesn't mean to say that ...

CAROL   Don't lie, you! I know you hate me. I've seen you
goin' home in your car, passin' us on the street. And
the way y' look at us. You hate all the kids.

She turns again to the sea, dismissing him.

BRIGGS   What ... makes you think that? Eh?

CAROL   Why can't I just stay out here, eh? Why can't I live
in one of them nice white houses an' do the garden
an' that?

BRIGGS Look ... Carol ... you're talking as though you've given up on life already. You sound as though life for you is just ending, instead of beginning. Now why can't, I mean, if it's what you want, what's to stop you working hard at school from now on, getting a good job and then moving out here when you're old enough? Eh?

CAROL (*She turns slowly to face him with a look of contempt.*) Don't be friggin' stupid.

(*She turns and looks down at the sea below.*)

It's been a great day today. I loved it. I don't wanna leave here an' go home.

(*She moves to the edge of the cliff.* BRIGGS *is alarmed but unable to move.*)

If I stayed though, it wouldn't be no good. You'd send the coppers to get me.

BRIGGS We'd have to. How would you survive out here?

CAROL I know.

(*pause*)

I'm not goin' back though.

BRIGGS Please ...

CAROL Sir, sir, y' know if you'd been my old feller, I woulda been all right, wouldn't I?

BRIGGS *slowly holds out his hand. She moves to the very edge of the cliff.* BRIGGS *is aware of how close she is.*

BRIGGS Carol. Carol, please come away from there. (*stretching out his hand to her*) Please.

CAROL *looks at him and a smile breaks across her face.*

CAROL Sir ... sir you don't half look funny, y' know.

BRIGGS (*smiling back at her*) Why?

CAROL Sir, you should smile more often, y' look great when y' smile.

BRIGGS   Come on, Carol.

He gingerly approaches her.

CAROL   What'll happen to me for doin' this, sir?

BRIGGS   Nothing. I promise you.

CAROL   Sir, y' promisin' now, but what about when we get back t' school?

BRIGGS   (*almost next to her now*) It won't be even mentioned.

She turns and looks down at the drop then back at BRIGGS'S *outstretched arm.* CAROL *lifts her hand to his. She slips.* BRIGGS *grabs out quickly and manages to pull her to him.* BRIGGS *wraps his arms around her.*

SCENE THIRTY-SIX **THE BEACH**

SUSAN *still waits anxiously on the beach whilst the* KIDS *play football. Other* KIDS *watch the game, including* LINDA *and* KAREN. REILLY *challenges* DIGGA *for the ball and gets it from him.*

KAREN   (*shouting*) Go on, Digga ... get him, get him.

LINDA   Come on, Brian.

REILLY *gets the ball past* DIGGA, *then around two more defenders, and scores.* LINDA *cheers;* REILLY *sees her and winks.* MRS KAY *and* COLIN *approach.* SUSAN *looks up in inquiry;* MRS KAY *shakes her head.* SUSAN *sighs.*

MRS KAY   (*as she approaches*) I think we'd better let the police know.

SUSAN   Shall I keep them playing ...

(*Behind* MRS KAY, SUSAN *can see* BRIGGS *and* CAROL *in the distance.*)

Oh, look ... he's found her.

MRS KAY   Oh, thank God.

She turns and starts hurrying towards them.

COLIN   I'll bet he makes a bloody meal of this.

SUSAN   I don't care as long as she's safe.

COLIN   Yeh, well, we'd better round them up. It'll be straight off now.

MRS KAY *approaches* CAROL *and* BRIGGS.

MRS KAY   Is she all right? Carol, the worry you've caused us!

BRIGGS   It's all right, Mrs Kay. I've dealt with all that.

MRS KAY   Where were you?

CAROL   On the cliff, miss.

MRS KAY   On the ...

BRIGGS   Mrs Kay, I've found her. Now will you just let me deal with this.

MRS KAY   (*She shakes her head as they walk up the beach towards the others.*) Carol Chandler.

BRIGGS   Right.

(*The main group are preparing to leave as* MRS KAY, CAROL *and* BRIGGS *reach them.*)

Right ... come on. Everyone on the coach.

(*General 'tuts' and moans of: 'Why can't we stay', etc.*)

Come on ... all of you, on.

SCENE THIRTY-SEVEN **THE COACH**

The staff stand by the coach doors as the KIDS *file by on to the coach.*

DRIVER   Right. (*to* BRIGGS) Back to the school then?

BRIGGS   School ... back to school?

(MRS KAY *looks up.*)

It's only early, isn't it?

(*to* MRS KAY) Anyway, you can't come all the way to the seaside and not pay a visit to the fair.

CAROL *overhears them as she climbs on to the coach. She rushes inside.*

CAROL   (*loud whisper*) We're going' the fair, we're goin' the
fair ... Sir's takin' us t' the fair.

The word is spread like fire inside the coach. Outside,
MRS KAY *is intrigued – half-smiling.*

BRIGGS   Play your cards right, I might take even you for a
ride on the waltzer.

SCENE THIRTY-EIGHT **A FAIRGROUND**

Rock and roll music. On the waltzer the KIDS,
including BRIGGS *and* CAROL *together in a car, are
spinning round.* MRS KAY *takes a photograph of* BRIGGS
and CAROL *climbing out of the waltzer car.* MRS KAY,
COLIN *and* SUSAN, REILLY *and* LINDA, DIGGA *and* KAREN,
ANDREWS, RONSON, CAROL *and some of the other* KIDS *are
all photographed in a group.* BRIGGS *is snapped eating
candy-floss, then again on the highest point of the big
wheel with mock fear on his face and* CAROL *next to
him her eyes closed in happy terror. Then he is
photographed playing darts, then with a cowboy hat
on handing a goldfish in a plastic bag to* CAROL.

SCENE THIRTY-NINE **BACK AT THE COACH**

As the KIDS *pile on to the coach,* BRIGGS, *still wearing
his cowboy hat, stands by the coach door.*

KIDS   (*as they get on to coach*)

Sir, thanks, sir.

Sir, that was Ace.

We had a great laugh, didn't we, sir?

Sir, we gonna come here again?

RONSON   Can we come tomorrow, sir?

BRIGGS   Oh, get on the bus, Ronson.

*Everyone is singing as the coach moves along. One of
the* KIDS *is collecting for the* DRIVER; REILLY *has his arm*

around LINDA; DIGGA *is with* KAREN; CAROL, *with her goldfish, sits next to* MRS KAY. RONSON *has a white mouse; the back seat is now occupied by* ANDREWS *and other* KIDS. BRIGGS *is also on the back seat – cowboy hat on, tie pulled down and singing with them.* MRS KAY *takes a photograph of them.*

MRS KAY Say 'Cheese'.

SCENE FORTY **BACK IN THE CITY**

The city can be seen out of the coach windows. Inside the coach the KIDS *are tired and worn out now. Some are sleeping, some are singing softly to themselves, some stare blankly out of the window.*

LINDA Y' glad y' came?

REILLY Yeh.

LINDA It was great wasn't it, eh?

REILLY It'll be the last one I go on.

LINDA Why?

REILLY Well I'm leaving in the summer aren't I?

LINDA What y' gonna do?

REILLY (*looking out of window*) Dunno.

(*Looks out of the window at the city.*) It's friggin' horrible when y' come back to it, isn't it?

LINDA What is?

REILLY That. (*nods at window*)

LINDA Oh, yeh. (*resigned*)

BRIGGS *with* ANDREWS *asleep next to him, sees the familiar surroundings and the kids hanging about in the streets. He sits up, puts his tie back to normal, goes to straighten his hair and feels the cowboy hat. He takes it off and puts it on* ANDREWS. *He then takes out a comb and combs his hair; puts on his jacket and walks down the aisle to* MRS KAY.

BRIGGS Well, nearly home.

MRS KAY (*She is taking the completed film from her camera.*) I've got some gems of you here. We'll have one of these up in the staff room when they're developed.

BRIGGS Eh? One of me?

MRS KAY Don't worry ... I'm not going to let you forget the day you enjoyed yourself.

BRIGGS (*He half laughs and watches her put the film into its box.*) Look ... why don't you give it to me to develop?

MRS KAY Would you?

BRIGGS Well, it would save you having to pay for it. I could do it in the lab.

MRS KAY (*handing it over*) I don't know, using school facilities for personal use.

He smiles at her and takes the film. He puts it in his pocket.

SCENE FORTY-ONE **OUTSIDE SCHOOL**

It is evening as the coach turns into the street outside the school and pulls up. BRIGGS *gets out, then the* KIDS *pour out shouting 'Tarars' and running up the street.* REILLY *and* LINDA *get off the coach together.*

BRIGGS Right! Come on, everyone out!

REILLY 'Night, sir. Enjoyed yourself today, didn't y', sir?

BRIGGS Pardon?

REILLY I didn't know you was like that, sir. Y' know, all right for a laugh an' that. See y' tomorrow sir.

BRIGGS Eh – Linda.

(*She stops.* BRIGGS *turns.*)

We'll, erm, we'll let the uniform go this time.

(*pause*)

But Linda, don't let me catch you dressing like that in the future, though.

She shrugs and walks off with REILLY. *The other* KIDS *make their way home.* MRS KAY *gets off the coach.*

MRS KAY   Nothing left behind. 'Night Ronny.

SUSAN   Good night.

The coach pulls away. The DRIVER *toots goodbye and they wave.*

MRS KAY   Ooh! ... That's that. I don't know about anyone else but I'm off for a drink.

COLIN   Oh, I'll second that.

SUSAN   Good idea.

MRS KAY   (*to* BRIGGS) You coming with us?

BRIGGS   (*The school looming behind him.*) Well, actually I've ...

SUSAN   Oh, come on ...

BRIGGS   No ... I'd better not. Thanks anyway. I've, um, lots of marking to do at home. Thanks all the same though.

MRS KAY   Oh well, if we can't twist your arm.

(*pause*)

Thanks for today.

She turns and goes to her car accompanied by SUSAN *and* COLIN. *She pulls away and toots goodbye.* BRIGGS *moves to his own car, puts his hand in his pocket and produces car keys and the roll of film. He looks at the film and then up at the school. He pulls open the film and exposes it to the light, crumples it up and puts it into his pocket. He then gets into his car, pulls away and at the junction turns right.* CAROL, *walking along the street with the goldfish in her grasp, looks up at the disappearing car.*

THE END

QUESTIONS AND EXPLORATIONS

1 Keeping Track

The questions in this section are designed to help your
reading and understanding of the play in the areas of plot,
character and interaction. They may be used as you read
the play or afterwards, for discussion or for writing. Some
are developed and expanded in the *Explorations* section.

Scenes 1–5

1 What image would we be given of the area of Liverpool
   in which the school is situated?

2 What do we learn about the nature of the Progress Class?

3 What impression are we given in these scenes of Mrs Kay?

4 What impression are we given of Mr Briggs?

5 How would an audience react to the conversation and
   interaction between Mrs Kay and Ronny Suttcliffe?

6 How does Mr Briggs's arrival alter the atmosphere on
   the coach?

Scene 6

7 What sorts of areas would the coach travel through as it
   leaves the city?

8 What impression are we given of Reilly and Digga?

9 How does Mr Briggs treat the various pupils to whom
   he speaks? How do they react?

10 What do we learn about Carol Chandler?

11 How is Mr Briggs affected by his conversation with
    Andrews?

12 How would Colin react to Linda's and Karen's advances?

Scenes 7–20

13 How would an audience react to the events at the first café in Scenes 7 to 12?

14 How would an audience react to the events at the second café in Scenes 13 to 20?

15 How would Mrs Kay and Mr Briggs each show their feelings about the other's attitudes in Scene 16?

Scene 21

16 What does Mr Briggs think of Mrs Kay's running of the trip? How would he do it differently?

17 How would Colin react to what Mr Briggs says to him?

18 How would Mr Briggs react to the news of the visit to the zoo?

Scenes 22–30

19 How do the children react to the animals in the zoo? Why?

20 Why does Mr Briggs decide that he can trust the children to 'act responsibly'?

21 What is the tone of the conversation between Mrs Kay and Mr Briggs in Scenes 25 and 27?

22 How should both Mrs Kay and Mr Briggs react to the children stealing the animals?

23 How would Mrs Kay show her reaction to Mr Briggs taking over the trip?

Scene 31

24 How would the kids with Mr Briggs show their boredom at the castle?

25 How would Linda and Karen behave towards Colin?

26 How would Carol and Andrews show their feelings in their conversation with Mrs Kay?

27 How have Mrs Kay's and Mr Briggs's feelings towards each other changed?

28 What, according to Mrs Kay, should education provide for the children in the Progress Class?

Scenes 32–34

29 What is the atmosphere amongst the children and the teachers on the beach?

30 How would Carol show her feelings to Mrs Kay in Scene 32?

31 How would Mrs Kay react to Carol?

32 How would Reilly react to Susan's advances? How would an audience react to this exchange?

33 How do the teachers react when they realise Carol is missing?

34 Why does Mr Briggs lose his temper with the other teachers?

Scene 35

35 How would Carol show how she feels on the cliff top?

36 How would Mr Briggs react on seeing her?

37 Why will Carol not leave the cliff edge?

38 How would Mr Briggs react to this?

39 How would Carol have been 'all right' if Mr Briggs had been her father?

40 How do Mr Briggs and Carol each feel, once he has saved her?

Scenes 36–39

41 How do Linda and Reilly now feel about each other?

42 What is Mr Briggs's attitude as he brings Carol back down to the beach?

43 How would Mrs Kay react to Mr Briggs's change in attitude?

44 What is the atmosphere at the fair?

45 What is the atmosphere on the coach afterwards?

Scenes 40 and 41

46 How, and why, do Reilly's and Linda's attitudes change?

47 How does Mr Briggs's attitude change as they return?

48 How have the children's attitude to Mr Briggs changed?

49 Why does Mr Briggs not go for a drink with the other teachers?

50 Why does Mr Briggs expose and ruin Mrs Kay's film?

51 What are Carol's feelings as Mr Briggs drives past her? How would they be shown?

52 What, finally, are the audience's feelings at the end of the play?

2 Explorations

The questions in this section are more detailed and rely upon your having read the whole play. Some of the questions develop ideas from the *Keeping Track* section. Because they tend to be more detailed, they offer the opportunity to develop the ideas into written, oral or practical coursework assignments. Some will require a close knowledge of the play; others will require a more imaginative response.

A Characters

Mrs Kay

1 'She always reminds me of a mother hen rather than a teacher'. Explain Mrs Kay's attitude to and manner with her pupils.

2 'That's the only rule we have today: think of yourselves but think of others as well'. What are Mrs Kay's aims in running the day out?

3 'You *are* on their side, aren't you?' Explain why Mrs Kay is on the Progress Class's side.

4 Write Mrs Kay's report for the Headmaster about the day out, drawing her conclusions about what the day achieved, if anything. Pay attention to character, attitude and style.

5 Create and script, or improvise, a Progress Class lesson led by Mrs Kay, either the following day or at a time of your choice. Ensure that characterisation and interaction are consistent with *Our Day Out*.

Mr Briggs

6 'You've got some real bright sparks here Mrs Kay. A right bunch'. Explain Mr Briggs's attitude and his manner with the pupils.

7 'Well I've learned a lesson today. Oh, yes, I have'. What lasting effects will the day out have upon Mr Briggs?

8 'You listen, Mr Briggs, you listen and perhaps you'll stop fooling yourself'. How is Mr Briggs fooling himself about the Progress Class? Is he right or wrong in his beliefs?

9 Write Mr Briggs's report for the Headmaster about the day out, drawing his conclusions about what the day achieved, if anything. Pay attention to character, attitude and style.

10 Create and script, or improvise, a Progress Class lesson led by Mr Briggs when Mrs Kay is absent: set it after the day out. Ensure that characterisation and interaction are consistent with the play.

Carol Chandler

11 'That's why we never have nothin' nice round our way – 'cos we'd just smash it up'. What type of neighbourhood and background does it seem that Carol comes from?

12 'I wanna stay here. Where it's nice'. What does Carol come to understand during the course of the day out? Why does she then climb the cliff alone?

13 Create and write what Carol would write about the day out on her return, either for herself at home in a diary, or as part of her work in the Progress Class. If you wish, write it as she herself would do so. Pay attention to character, attitude and style.

14 Create and script, or improvise, a scene between Carol, Mrs Kay and Mr Briggs at school the day after the day out. How would the teachers show their attitudes to her, and how would she show her attitude to them?

15 Create and script, or improvise, the scene in Carol's home when she returns and tries to tell her family about her day out.

The Progress Class

16 'You've got some real bright sparks here, Mrs Kay'. Explain the function of the Progress Class. Is it fair that these pupils should be put together in such a class?

17 'It's too late for them … we're not going to solve anything today'. What are Mrs Kay's priorities in her work with the Progress Class?

18 'It's friggin' horrible when y' come back to it, isn't it?' What, overall, do the members of the Progress Class have to look forward to in life?

19 Select one member of the Progress Class. Write the report on the day out that s/he would write the next day. Pay attention to character, attitude and style of writing fully in rôle if appropriate.

20 Create, or improvise, a Progress Class lesson the day after the day out in which the class reflects on its trip. Pay attention to characterisation and interaction, ensuring that they are consistent with the play.

General

21 Select two of the following: Les, Colin or Susan, Ronny Suttcliffe, Mac or John, Ronson or Andrews. How does Russell create and convey their characters? What are their functions in the play?

22 Create and script, or improvise, a scene in the school's staff room the following day. Create other characters' attitudes and opinions now that the trip is over. Ensure that characterisation and interaction are consistent with the play.

23 Create and script, or improvise, a scene which shows a mealtime in one of the following homes: Carol's, Reilly's or Mr Briggs's.

Using your understanding of character and background, and creating other characters if necessary, show how the meal would be conducted. Use dialogue and stage directions as appropriate.

B Themes

1 'You *are* on their side, aren't you?' What does Willy Russell intend the audience to think of Mrs Kay and her attitude to education?

2 'You listen, Mr Briggs, you listen and perhaps you'll stop fooling yourself'. What does Willy Russell intend the audience to think of Mr Briggs and his attitude to education?

3 What, according to Russell, should schooling and education offer to pupils like those in the Progress Class?

4 'I wanna stay here. Where it's nice'. What future do the pupils in the Progress Class have to look forward to?

5 What solutions, if any, could be proposed in order to improve the situation of pupils like these in the Progress Class?

C In Presentation

1 Select one of the major characters. What aspects of her/his character would you need as an actor to highlight for the benefit of an audience? How would you use voice/gesture/ movement to achieve this?

2 Select two contrasting characters. Design their costumes so that the nature of the characters would be clearly conveyed to an audience.

3 Select a sequence of scenes. What sorts of locations would you choose to use as settings for these scenes in a filmed version of the play? What qualities would you seek to convey to your audience through these settings?

4 Select either one of the humorous scenes or one of the confrontations between Mrs Kay and Mr Briggs. Suggest how, using voice, gesture and interaction, you would realise the scene's potential for the benefit of an audience.

5 Select a scene or a sequence of successive scenes. How would you set about adapting those scenes for a staged presentation?

D Criticism

1 How accurate and effective is Willy Russell's presentation of a school trip in *Our Day Out*? How does he achieve this?

2 What, in your opinion, does Willy Russell passionately want to communicate in *Our Day Out*? How successfully does he achieve his intentions?

3 'Mr Russell gives his audience a day out but leaves his characters stranded'. How, and why, are the characters in the play stranded?

4 With whom does Willy Russell intend the audience to sympathise and identify, Mrs Kay or Mr Briggs? Give reasons and evidence from the play for your answer.

5 'I believe that every play I have ever written has, ultimately, been one which celebrates the goodness of man ...'. What is the goodness that Willy Russell celebrates in *Our Day Out*? How would the audience feel at the end of the play?

FURTHER READING

In addition to *Our Day Out*, the following plays by Willy Russell are well worth reading or seeing:

Stags and Hens
Educating Rita } Published in one volume by
Blood Brothers Methuen 1986

Shirley Valentine Methuen 1992

The first major study of Willy Russell, consisting principally of an extended interview with the author, is

Willy Russell and his Plays   John Gill   Countyvise 1992